ASEAN+3 MULTI-CURRENCY BOND ISSUANCE FRAMEWORK

IMPLEMENTATION GUIDELINES FOR CAMBODIA

DECEMBER 2020

Some rights reserved. Published in 2020.

ISBN 978-92-9262-568-9 (print), 978-92-9262-569-6 (electronic), 978-92-9262-570-2 (ebook)
ISSN 2616-4663 (print), 2616-4671 (electronic)
Publication Stock No. TCS 200385-2
DOI: http://dx.doi.org/10.22617/TCS200385-2

The views expressed in this publication are those of the authors and do not necessarily reflect the views and policies of the Asian Development Bank (ADB) or its Board of Governors or the governments they represent.

ADB does not guarantee the accuracy of the data included in this publication and accepts no responsibility for any consequence of their use. The mention of specific companies or products of manufacturers does not imply that they are endorsed or recommended by ADB in preference to others of a similar nature that are not mentioned.

By making any designation of or reference to a particular territory or geographic area, or by using the term "economy" in this document, ADB does not intend to make any judgments as to the legal or other status of any territory or area.

Please contact pubsmarketing@adb.org if you have questions or comments with respect to content, or if you wish to obtain copyright permission for your intended use that does not fall within these terms, or for permission to use the ADB logo.

Corrigenda to ADB publications may be found at http://www.adb.org/publications/corrigenda.

Notes:
In this report, international standards for naming conventions—International Organization for Standardization (ISO) 3166 for economy codes and ISO 4217 for currency codes—are used to reflect the discussions of the ASEAN+3 Bond Market Forum to promote and support implementation of international standards in financial transactions in the region. ASEAN+3 comprises the Association of Southeast Asian Nations (ASEAN) plus the People's Republic of China, Japan, and the Republic of Korea.

The economies of ASEAN+3 as defined in ISO 3166 include Brunei Darussalam (BN; BRN); Cambodia (KH; KHM); the People's Republic of China (CN; CHN); Hong Kong, China (HK; HKG); Indonesia (ID; IDN); Japan (JP; JPN); the Republic of Korea (KR; KOR); the Lao People's Democratic Republic (LA; LAO); Malaysia (MY; MYS); Myanmar (MM; MMR); the Philippines (PH; PHL); Singapore (SG; SGP); Thailand (TH; THA); and Viet Nam (VN; VNM).

The currencies of ASEAN+3 as defined in ISO 4217 include the Brunei dollar (BND), Cambodian riel (KHR), Chinese renminbi (CNY), Hong Kong dollar (HKD), Indonesian rupiah (IDR), Japanese yen (JPY), Korean won (KRW), Lao kip (LAK), Malaysian ringgit (MYR), Myanmar kyat (MMK), Philippine peso (PHP), Singapore dollar (SGD), Thai baht (THB), and Vietnamese dong (VND).

Contents

Tables and Figure

Tables

Figure

Foreword

The ASEAN+3 Bond Market Forum (ABMF) proposed the ASEAN+3 Multi-Currency Bond Issuance Framework (AMBIF) in 2014.[1] The following year, AMBIF's definition, purpose, and underlying practices were published.

The objective of AMBIF is to enable issuers in ASEAN+3 to issue bonds, notes, or *sukuk* (Islamic bonds) in the professional market or market segment of any participating economy in a comparable manner, using the same or similar practices and a standardized approach to disclosure. This, in turn, allows for a streamlined approval process (where required), lower costs, and faster time-to-market. The underlying incentive of AMBIF, pursuant to the original mandate of ABMF, was to improve intra-regional bond transactions in ASEAN+3.

AMBIF itself does not change a market's legal or regulatory framework. Instead, AMBIF employs the existing characteristics of each economy's professional bond market by using those features comparable to the AMBIF Elements, which are a normalized set of underlying requirements for eligible issuances. Issuer and investor criteria, place of issuance, and currency considerations are part of the AMBIF Elements. One key element is the creation and use of the Single Submission Form as the single common document for information disclosure across all AMBIF markets.

The AMBIF Implementation Guidelines for each participating market are provided to review the AMBIF Elements and detail the corresponding features of the participating market in relation to each element. Following the proven approach for output created by ABMF, the AMBIF Implementation Guidelines have been reviewed and their contents approved by each market's respective regulatory authorities so that interested parties, particularly issuers and their service providers, can pursue further issuances under AMBIF with ease and certainty.

This document explains the AMBIF Elements; puts into perspective the corresponding features of the professional Cambodia bond market; highlights market characteristics that are significant for issuers and investors; and reviews the regulatory processes required for different types of issuances of debt securities, including for both resident and nonresident issuers, and for different issuer types.

Yasuyuki Sawada
Chief Economist and Director General
Economic Research and Regional Cooperation Department
Asian Development Bank

---

[1] ASEAN+3 refers to the 10 members of the Association of Southeast Asian Nations (ASEAN) plus the People's Republic of China, Japan, and the Republic of Korea.

Acknowledgments

The ASEAN+3 Multi-Currency Bond Issuance Framework (AMBIF) Implementation Guidelines for the original participating markets were first published in 2015 as part of the Phase 2 Report of the ASEAN+3 Bond Market Forum (ABMF). Across the region, domestic bond markets have experienced tremendous development over the past 5 years, which also allowed additional markets, such as Cambodia, to consider participation in AMBIF. Now in Phase 3, ABMF would like to share, in the public domain, information on these developments by publishing the AMBIF Implementation Guidelines for Cambodia for the first time, with a particular focus on market features that represent, or influence, AMBIF Elements in Cambodia.

The ABMF Sub-Forum 1 team—comprising Satoru Yamadera (principal financial sector specialist, Economic Research and Regional Cooperation Department [ERCD], Asian Development Bank [ADB]); Kosintr Puongsophol (financial sector specialist, ERCD, ADB); and ADB consultants Shigehito Inukai and Matthias Schmidt, together with ABMF International Expert Hirohiko Suzuki—would like to stress the significance and magnitude of the contributions made by ABMF national members and experts for Cambodia, including the Cambodia Securities Exchange, National Bank of Cambodia, and Securities and Exchange Commission of Cambodia. These policy bodies, regulatory authorities, and market institutions generously gave their time for market visit meetings, discussions, and follow-up. They have also reviewed and provided inputs on the draft AMBIF Implementation Guidelines for Cambodia over the course of ABMF Phase 3.

Particular mention should also be made of SBI Royal Securities, which provided regular input into the compilation of these Implementation Guidelines from a domestic perspective.

No part of this report represents the official views or opinions of any institution that participated in this activity as an ABMF member, observer, or expert. The ABMF Sub-Forum 1 team bears sole responsibility for the contents of this report.

ASEAN+3 Bond Market Forum

Abbreviations

ABMF	ASEAN+3 Bond Market Forum
ADB	Asian Development Bank
AMBIF	ASEAN+3 Multi-Currency Bond Issuance Framework
ASEAN	Association of Southeast Asian Nations
ASEAN+3	Association of Southeast Asian Nations plus the People's Republic of China, Japan, and the Republic of Korea
CRA	credit rating agency
CSA	cash settlement agent
CSD	central securities depository
CSX	Cambodia Securities Exchange
FCY	foreign currency
KHR	Cambodian riel (ISO code)
MTN	medium-term note
NBC	National Bank of Cambodia
SECC	Securities and Exchange Commission of Cambodia
SF1	Sub-Forum 1 of ABMF
SSF	Single Submission Form
USD	United States dollar (ISO code)

USD1 = KHR4,100 (as of 30 September 2020)[2]

---

[2] Official exchange rate on the website of the National Bank of Cambodia.
https://www.nbc.org.kh/english/economic_research/exchange_rate.php.

AMBIF Elements in Cambodia

This chapter describes the key features of the ASEAN+3 Multi-Currency Bond Issuance Framework (AMBIF), also known as the AMBIF Elements, and puts into perspective the equivalent or prospective features of the domestic corporate bond market in Cambodia.

Please note that the descriptions in these Implementation Guidelines are temporary, as it is expected that further regulations may be issued after a few pilot issues. The Implementation Guidelines will conform to the existing domestic regulations, as all bonds will be issued based on domestic regulations.

A.   Summary of AMBIF Elements

AMBIF issuances in Cambodia will be considered Debt Securities Offerings to Qualified Investors, making use of the professional investor concept introduced in 2016, and the AMBIF Single Submission Form (SSF). The Securities and Exchange Commission of Cambodia (SECC) considers the SSF to be the key application and disclosure document for Debt Securities Offerings to Qualified Investors and may request to augment the SSF information, if so deemed necessary.[1]

Debt Securities Offerings to Qualified Investors are described pursuant to the Prakas on Debt Securities Offering to Qualified Investors, promulgated by the SECC in May 2020, but they are not the same as the issuance method described as private placement in law and regulations.[2] Private placement remains a separate issuance method for no more than 30 investors; while only requiring a notification to the SECC, this issuance method does not carry prescriptions of disclosure of any kind or the need for terms and conditions and, hence, does not fulfill the expectations of an AMBIF market.

Table 1 identifies the features and practices of the domestic corporate bond market in Cambodia that directly correspond or are equivalent to the AMBIF Elements.

---

[1] The language follows the understanding of the Sub-Forum 1 of ABMF (SF1) team that the SECC has, in principle, no objections to accepting the SSF as the key application and disclosure document for Debt Securities Offerings to Qualified Investors. The SECC Legal Department may review the SSF from time to time for any necessary inclusions.

[2] The text of the Prakas, like other relevant Prakas, will eventually be available in English and Khmer language from the website of the SECC at http://www.secc.gov.kh/english/m23.php?pn=3.

Table 1: AMBIF Elements and Equivalent Features in Cambodia

AMBIF Element	Description	Equivalent Feature
Domestic Settlement	Securities are settled at a national CSD in each ASEAN+3 market.	Settlement occurs at CSX as the operator of clearing and settlement facilities approved by the SECC.
Harmonized Documents for Submission (Single Submission Form)	There is a common approach to submitting information as an input to regulatory process(es) where approval or consent is required; appropriate disclosure information, based on an ADRB recommendation, needs to be included.	The SECC considers the SSF to be the key disclosure document for Debt Securities Offerings to Qualified Investors.
Registration or Profile Listing in ASEAN+3 (Place of Continuous Disclosure)	Information on bonds, notes, and issuer needs to be disclosed continuously in the relevant ASEAN+3 market. A registration or listing authority function is required to ensure continuous and quality disclosure.	Listing on CSX is mandatory and subject to the CSX Debt Securities Listing Rules.
Currency	Bonds or notes are denominated in one of the currencies normally used for issuances in the domestic bond market of an ASEAN+3 member.	Cambodian riel, possibly US dollar[a]
Scope of Issuers	Resident of an ASEAN+3 member	Presently, limited to resident issuers
Scope of Investors	Professional investors defined in accordance with the applicable laws, regulations, or market practice in each market in ASEAN+3	Qualified Investors, as prescribed in SECC regulations, including foreign investors

ADRB = AMBIF Documentation Recommendation Board; AMBIF = ASEAN+3 Multi-Currency Bond Issuance Framework; ASEAN+3 = Association of Southeast Asian Nations plus the People's Republic of China, Japan, and the Republic of Korea; CSD = central securities depository; CSX = Cambodia Securities Exchange; FCY = foreign currency; SECC = Securities and Exchange Commission of Cambodia; US = United States.
[a] For issuances denominated in US dollars, an inquiry to the SECC may be necessary.
Source: ABMF SF1.

B.   Description of AMBIF Elements and Equivalent Features in Cambodia

The market features in Cambodia that are comparable to the AMBIF Elements listed in Table 1 are explained in this section in greater detail.

1.   Domestic Settlement

ASEAN+3 Multi-Currency Bond Issuance Framework

AMBIF is aimed at supporting the domestic bond markets of ASEAN+3 member economies. To be recognized as a domestic bond, an AMBIF bond or note needs to be settled at the designated central securities depository (CSD). Hence, domestic settlement is a key feature of an AMBIF bond.

Equivalent Features in Cambodia

With the Cambodian capital market at a nascent stage, there is no CSD yet. At present, publicly offered securities are to be listed on the Cambodia Securities Exchange (CSX), and subsequent trades in such listed securities are then cleared and settled at CSX, as the operator of clearing and settlement facilities approved by the SECC. In this capacity, CSX settles the securities side of trades, while the cash side is settled through cash settlement agents who are participants of the clearing and settlement facility operated by CSX.

CSX currently also holds the approval, as the operator of a securities depository, to perform the safekeeping function for listed securities, including corporate debt securities. Please also see Chapter II.J for a detailed description of asset safekeeping in Cambodia.

For the purpose of AMBIF, the current process fulfills the requirement of domestic settlement.

2.   Harmonized Documents for Submission (Single Submission Form)

ASEAN+3 Multi-Currency Bond Issuance Framework

Based on the review of actual offering circulars, information memoranda, and program information formats in ASEAN+3, it was recognized that most information was similar or comparable. Hence, a Single Submission Form (SSF)—a single format in English that can be applied to all of the relevant regulatory processes for bond or note issuance in each participating ASEAN+3 market—was proposed. The information contained in the SSF has been normalized based on the prevailing regulations in each participating market, and therefore can be accepted by all relevant regulatory authorities and market institutions for their respective approvals or consent in anticipation of an AMBIF bond or note issuance.

Equivalent Features in Cambodia

The SECC considers the SSF as the key disclosure document for Debt Securities Offerings to Qualified Investors. The inclusion of specific content required by the SECC may be necessary in the future and would become part of the standard SSF template.

Under the current regulatory framework, the SECC does not define a specific format for the application and disclosure document(s) to be submitted and, consequently, the

SECC could consider any form and format on its merits, provided that the disclosure information requirements imposed by the SECC, specifically those prescribed for Debt Securities Offerings to Qualified Investors, are met. In any case, the SECC may request additional information to be submitted in the process of reviewing an issuance application.

At this point, the SSF needs to be translated into Khmer at the final stage, though both the English and Khmer versions will be treated equally by the SECC and an English-only SSF can be used at the working stage. If both English and Khmer versions of the SSF are used, the issuer must ensure that the information contained in both versions is equivalent.[3]

During the listing application process, CSX accepts the SSF as the key disclosure document when registered by the SECC. The SSF will need to be in Khmer, following the present requirement set by the SECC. At the time of listing eligibility review, CSX will accept a draft SSF in English as a working document.

To allow the SSF to act as both issuance and listing application, as well as key disclosure document, changes to the existing SECC regulations and CSX Listing Rules would have to be made. For the time being, an application form separate from the SSF is required for both the issuance and listing application process (see also the detailed description of the application and approval process in Chapter III).

3.   Registration or Profile Listing in ASEAN+3 (Place of Continuous Disclosure)

ASEAN+3 Multi-Currency Bond Issuance Framework

Information on the issuer and the bond or note needs to be disclosed continuously in ASEAN+3 markets. A registration or listing authority function to ensure continuous disclosure is required. This will also ensure the quality of information disclosure and help create a transparent, well-organized market for AMBIF issuances that is differentiated from ordinary private placements or exempt offers for which information is often neither available nor guaranteed. Owing to this important feature, an AMBIF secondary market is expected to emerge as the number of issuances increases.

A profile listing is a listing without trading. The objective of a profile listing is to make an issuer and a bond or note visible, and to provide more information to investors via a recognized listing place, particularly those investors with more restrictive mandates such as mutual and pension funds. A profile listing at a designated listing place can ensure the flow of continuous disclosure information and possibly even reference pricing in some markets.

Equivalent Features in Cambodia

Debt Securities Offerings to Qualified Investors need to be listed on CSX, subject to the fulfillment of prevailing eligibility criteria and listing requirements. The listing is subject to the Debt Securities Listing Rules and CSX approval.

Article 3 of the CSX Market Operation Rules states that securities listed on CSX have to be traded on CSX (i.e., not traded elsewhere). Investors may choose not to trade their debt securities (e.g., in the case of a buy-and-hold strategy), but should investors decide to sell, such trades must be done on CSX.

---

[3] In the case of a dispute, the court will decide whether the Khmer and/or English version will be used as a basis for passing judgment; it is likely to be the Khmer version, since otherwise a translation would not be required.

The listing on CSX will ensure transparency of the initial disclosure information and continuous disclosure information, in line with the continuous disclosure requirements set by the SECC and CSX. In any case, the supervision and enforcement of continuous disclosure obligations by the issuers of bonds or notes in Cambodia, including those for Debt Securities Offerings to Qualified Investors, remain with the SECC.

CSX accepts the submission of continuous disclosure information in both Khmer and English.

Given the early stage of bond market development in Cambodia, the listing on CSX fulfills the intention of the Registration or Profile Listing feature under AMBIF.

4. Currency

ASEAN+3 Multi-Currency Bond Issuance Framework

In the context of AMBIF, the denomination of a bond or note is expected to be the currency normally issued in the domestic bond markets of ASEAN+3 (i.e., the local currency of that particular market). This does not exclude the possibility of issuing in other currencies if market practice regularly supports these other currencies and if cash-clearing capabilities exist. At present, the United States (US) dollar (ISO code: USD), Japanese yen (ISO code: JPY), and offshore Chinese renminbi (ISO code: CNH) are the other currencies most commonly in use in ASEAN+3 markets.

Equivalent Features in Cambodia

At the time of compilation of these Implementation Guidelines, Debt Securities Offerings to Qualified Investors could be issued in Cambodian riels or US dollars.

5. Scope of Issuers

ASEAN+3 Multi-Currency Bond Issuance Framework

As AMBIF aims to support the development of domestic bond and note markets in the region and promote the intra-regional recycling of funds, an issuer must be a resident of ASEAN+3.

Equivalent Features in Cambodia

The regulatory framework for the corporate bond market in Cambodia does make mention of resident issuers in some provisions. At the same time, nonresident issuers are not specifically excluded from the market, and their participation would be subject to approval by the SECC.

Resident issuers include private and listed corporate entities, as well as state-owned enterprises. Banks and financial institutions licensed and supervised by the National Bank of Cambodia (NBC) are able to issue and list debt securities, as stipulated in the Prakas on Conditions for Banking and Financial Institutions for Application to be Listed on the Cambodia Securities Exchange, issued by the NBC on 27 September 2017.

6. Scope of Investors

ASEAN+3 Multi-Currency Bond Issuance Framework

Professional investors are defined in accordance with regulations and/or practice in each market in ASEAN+3. Some jurisdictions may have a clear definition of professional investors, while other jurisdictions may need to establish the concept through agreements.

Professional investors are institutions defined by law and licensed or otherwise registered with regulators by law in their economy of domicile and, hence, are subject to governance and inspection based on securities market and/or prudential regulations. Most of them are also subject to oversight and professional conduct and best practice rules by a self-regulatory organization such as an exchange or a market association.

Equivalent Features in Cambodia

The SECC issued the Prakas on Qualified Investors in the Securities Sector (see also Appendix 3) in August 2016. With the publication of this *Prakas*, the SECC introduced to the market the Qualified Investors concept, which distinguishes between defined investor types and sets their eligibility and qualifying criteria. Like all *Prakas* issued by the SECC, its text is available for download as a PDF document—in both Khmer and English—from the SECC website.[4]

Foreign institutional investors are eligible to be considered Qualified Investors as long as they fall into any of the investor types specified under Institutional Investors.

All investors in the Cambodian securities market will need to obtain an investor ID prior to commencing their buying of securities (see Chapter II.G for details).

Qualified Investors

The Prakas on Qualified Investors in the Securities Sector introduced and defined the terms Qualified Investor, Institutional Investor, and High Net-Worth Investor to the securities market in Cambodia. Qualified Investors may be Institutional Investors or High Net-Worth Investors.

According to Article 3 of the Prakas on Qualified Investors in the Securities Sector, the eligibility criteria to be considered as Qualified Investors are as follows:

Institutional Investors include

    i.   the NBC;
    ii. securities firms and investment advisors that have obtained licenses from the SECC;
    iii. collective investment scheme dealers that have obtained licenses from the SECC;
    iv. banking and financial institutions that have obtained licenses from the NBC;
    v. insurance companies that have obtained licenses from the Ministry of Economy and Finance;
    vi. the National Social Security Fund, the National Fund for Veterans, Persons with Disabilities Foundation, and the National Social Security Fund for Civil Servants;
    vii. international financial institutions that have obtained an approval from the Director General of the SECC;
    viii. financial institutions development funds that have obtained an approval from the Director General of the SECC; and

---

[4] See
http://www.secc.gov.kh/boards/index.php?bid=m23Prakas&nav=download&no=32&file=2&md=&u=L2JvYXJkcy9pbmRleC5waHA/YmlkPW0yM1ByYWthcyZuYXY9cmVhZCZudGb2RlPXIlYWQmbm89MzImc2IxJn
NjaD0mc2NoX3R5cGU9JnNjaF9zZXk9JmNhdGU9.

ix. other legal entities that have obtained an approval from the Director
     General of the SECC.

High Net-Worth Investors include:

i.   legal entities fulfilling one of the following criteria:

     a. total shareholders' equity of at least KHR2 billion as per the latest
         financial statement,
     b. annual revenue of at least KHR500 million in the last 2 years, or
     c. at least KHR200 million of investments in the securities sector in
         Cambodia; and

ii. any individual who aims to register as a Qualified Investor and, together
     with a spouse (if any), fulfills the following criteria:

     a. total net assets of at least KHR1 billion,
     b. annual income of at least KHR80 million, or
     c. investment participation in the securities sector in Cambodia of at least
         KHR100 million.

Institutional Investors will need to submit official documents and other necessary
information stating their eligibility to the securities firms before they can be
registered as such. High Net-Worth Investors are required to complete a form set
by the securities firm and approved by the Director General of the SECC, and
attach bank statements, investment reports, or similar documents confirming their
compliance with the qualifying criteria mentioned above.

The securities firms are required to verify the information provided by the intended
investors who request to be Qualified Investors and submit a list of such Qualified
Investors to the SECC on a periodic basis after having ascertained that the
qualifications are still being met.

AMBIF Bond and Note Issuance: Relevant Features in Cambodia

In addition to market features corresponding to the AMBIF Elements, a number of general Cambodian market features for bond and note issuance to Qualified Investors need to be considered by market participants. These features are described in this chapter.

A.   Governing Law and Jurisdiction

Governing law and the jurisdiction for specific service provisions in relation to a bond or note issuance may have some relevance in the context of AMBIF. Potential issuers may consider issuing under the laws or jurisdiction of an economy or market other than the place of issuance. The choice of governing law or the contractual preferences of stakeholders can affect accessibility to a specific investor universe that may otherwise not be accessible if a bond or note were issued under the laws of the place of issuance. However, provisions related to bond or note issuance and settlement must be governed by the laws and regulations of the place of issuance since an AMBIF bond is a domestic bond.

The Kingdom of Cambodia's legal system follows the civil law tradition. In Cambodia, the governing law and the jurisdiction of agreements by contracting parties are required to be Cambodian law and the Kingdom of Cambodia, respectively. At the same time, while a request for the use of another law or jurisdiction has not yet been received, the SECC may offer some flexibility, such as consideration on a case-by-case basis for issuers to use the laws or jurisdictions of countries for which it has entered into a memorandum of understanding with the respective securities market regulatory authorities. It is likely that taxation considerations will also play a role in the SECC review and decision.

If law other than Cambodian law is chosen as the governing law in the transaction documents, the parties thereto may choose a specific jurisdiction of a court in which disputes will be adjudicated. However, if bonds or notes are issued denominated in Cambodian riel, Cambodian law should normally be used to govern issuance and settlement related issues, regardless of governing law(s) of other matters.

Notwithstanding the above, the Cambodian courts and courts of other jurisdictions may have jurisdiction over disputes arising in relation to such bond issuances, to the extent permitted by Cambodian or other relevant laws.

In any case, the actual use of governing laws or jurisdictions other than those of Cambodia may be subject to clarification or legal advice from a qualified law firm, as may be necessary.

B.   Language of Documentation and Disclosure Items

It is envisaged that most ASEAN+3 markets participating in AMBIF will accept the use of a common document in English. However, some markets may require the submission of approval-related information in their prescribed format and in the local language. In such cases, concessions from the regulatory authorities for a submission of required information in English—in addition to the local language and formats—may be sought.

Presently, all contracts, applications for securities issuance and listing, licensing or accreditation approvals, and securities-issuance-related documentation and disclosure items, as well as correspondence with regulatory authorities and market institutions (if so required), must be in Khmer, which is the official language of the Kingdom of Cambodia.

During the application for the issuance of securities, the SECC requires all relevant contracts in relation to such issuance to be submitted (see also Chapter III.B.1 for details). According to provisions in the Anukret on the Implementation of the Law on Issuance and Trading of Non-Government Securities (No. 54 ANKR BK), contracts that are not originally written in Khmer shall be attached and also translated into Khmer by persons recognized by the SECC.

From a practical perspective, it should be assumed that contracts entered into between an issuer and the domestic agents required in the context of a bond or note issuance, such as bondholders representative, cash settlement agent, and securities registrar, will be written and executed in Khmer (see also next section).

At the same time, the disclosure document for the issuance of debt securities may also be in English. It may be produced first in English, as long as the final version of the disclosure document will be available in Khmer at the time the offer of debt securities commences. In any case, the issuer will be required to maintain equivalency of information between document versions in both languages.

The SECC is presently studying whether an application form in Khmer and supporting documents in English may be acceptable.

During the listing eligibility review (the process is explained in Chapter III), CSX accepts draft or working copies of key disclosure and supplementary documents in English, including the SSF. Legally binding contracts and other material information need to be submitted to CSX in Khmer.

For the listing application, the key disclosure document that was registered by the SECC, such as the SSF, will need to be submitted to CSX and has to be in Khmer. While the Listing Application Form itself contains text in both Khmer and English, it will need to be completed in Khmer, as per current CSX requirements.

CSX already accepts and displays initial and continuous disclosure information in both English and Khmer (as available) on its website.

C.   Official and Market Documentation

Parties involved in a bond or note issuance in Cambodia are required to submit a number of official documents and/or execute contracts or agreements that govern the relationships between the service providers and the issuer and investors, respectively. These documents and contracts or agreements are required for normal market issuances and for issuances under AMBIF. However, these Implementation Guidelines only detail the official documents and market documentation for an AMBIF issuance.

Applicable market documentation can be distinguished between official documents for submission by the issuer to authorities and market institutions, and those market documents to be concluded by the issuer or other parties with their service providers.

1.   Official Documents

Key among the official documents for an AMBIF issuance are the application form and the key disclosure document for the issuance to be submitted to the SECC, and the Listing Application Form and agreement to be submitted to CSX.

a.   Issuance Application Form (to SECC)

The issuance application form is a format mentioned in regulations and specified by the SECC as the cover letter for the issuance application for debt instruments in the Cambodian market. The issuance application form will need to be completed in Khmer and is to be accompanied by the key disclosure document and other supporting documents, as stipulated in the Prakas on Debt Securities Offering to Qualified Investors.

b.   Key Disclosure Document (Single Submission Form)

The SECC considers the SSF as the key disclosure document for AMBIF issuances in Cambodia. The SSF is a template document created and maintained by ABMF. Appendix 1 of these Implementation Guidelines contains a link to the latest version of the SSF.

The SSF template is based on the style and format of an information memorandum, the standard documentation used in international bond markets for bond and note offers to professional investors. The SSF has been normalized by ABMF across the ASEAN+3 markets participating in AMBIF and contains common issuer and issuance information and disclosure information, plus some additional information specifically required in selected markets only.[7]

The SSF is created and maintained in English to achieve maximum reusability for an issuer tapping a number of AMBIF markets. Please also see section B for details on the language of official documents in Cambodia.

c.   Listing Application Form (to CSX)

The Listing Application Form is an official form provided by CSX that is to be submitted at the beginning of the listing approval process and is a separate document from the key disclosure document (see item b). Please see Chapter III for a complete description of the regulatory process for an AMBIF issuance, including listing.

The Listing Application Form contains text in both the Khmer language and English, but has to be completed in Khmer. The form is to be signed and stamped by the issuer and underwriter, and submitted in physical form in duplicate.

The Listing Application Form needs to be obtained from CSX, and is presently not available for download from the CSX website.

---

[7] At the time of the compilation of these Implementation Guidelines, the participating economies included Cambodia; Hong Kong, China; Japan; Malaysia; the Philippines; Singapore; and Thailand.

d.   Securities Listing Agreement

The issuer will need to sign a Securities Listing Agreement with CSX prior to the listing of an AMBIF issue taking effect. The Securities Listing Agreement is an existing standard contract provided by CSX in the Khmer language and approved by the SECC.

2.   Market Documentation

Market documentation refers to documents or contracts that are to be concluded between the issuer or investors and their service providers. Some of these documents are part of the supporting documents or attachments to official documents during the issuance and listing approval process.

a.   Bondholders Representative Agreement

A bondholders representative acts on behalf of the investors in the context of a bond or note, but is appointed by the issuer. The appointment of a bondholders representative is only mandatory for Debt Securities Offerings to all Qualified Investors (i.e., both Institutional Investors and High Net-Worth Investor); if the offering is aimed at Institutional Investors only, the appointment of a bondholders representative is optional. Please see section G for a full description of the bondholders representative function.

To appoint a bondholders representative, the issuer and the selected bondholders representative need to enter into a Bondholders Representative Agreement. The agreement sets out the duties of the bondholders representative and its rights and obligations under SECC provisions. The agreement also compels the issuer to provide regular information to the bondholders representative and comply with SECC prescriptions. The Bondholders Representative Agreement and its contents should be expected to follow Cambodian law as governing law.

Under the current regulatory framework for the corporate bond market, the Bondholders Representative Agreement, if executed, is to be submitted to the SECC as a supporting document to the issuance application form, as well as to CSX when completing the listing application. As a material contract, the Bondholders Representative Agreement is required to be submitted to the SECC and CSX in Khmer.

In a mature market, the Bondholders Representative Agreement is typically provided by the service provider (a commercial bank or securities firm) offering the services of a bondholders representative; the agreement is usually in the form of a template, which may be subject to negotiation within the regulatory framework and completion based on mutual requirements and understanding.

b.   Client Agreement or Custody Agreement

Professional investors, which in Cambodia are referred to as Qualified Investors, often have very specific requirements for the safekeeping and settlement of their investment assets and associated services. Many professional investors are subject to prudential regulations in their home market, which contain prescriptions on types of investments, asset safety, and limitations of risk.

To comply with these provisions, professional investors must actively seek the services of custodians in the markets they invest in. The absence of a dedicated custodian function, or an underlying agreement for the provision of such function, may be cause not to pursue investments in a given market, particularly for foreign institutional investors.

In Cambodia and in the context of AMBIF, the client agreement, which internationally is also termed a custody agreement, is a contract to be entered into between a Qualified Investor (resident or nonresident) and a service provider accredited as a custodian agent by the SECC. In the absence of accredited custodian agents, the function of a custodian agent can also be performed by other parties who are participants in the designated depository for corporate debt securities in Cambodia (i.e., securities firms). If so, the securities firm would enter into a custody agreement with the investor. Please also see section J in this chapter on the present asset safekeeping practices and future custodian agent service.

A custody agreement is typically provided as a template by the custodian or securities firm, and the contents negotiated or finalized between investor and custodian, depending on the service level required by the investor and the service capabilities available from the custodian.

For reference, Article 22 of the Prakas on the Accreditation of the Custodian Agent in the Securities Sector details the content expectations set by the SECC.

c.   Underwriting Agreement

The issuer will need to enter into an underwriting agreement, with an underwriter licensed by the SECC, prior to an issuance application to the SECC. The underwriting agreement, or an engagement letter, is considered the designated supporting document for such an issuance application, as well as for the listing application to CSX.

The underwriting agreement is typically provided by the underwriter to the issuer, commensurate with the agreed provision of a firm or best-effort underwriting commitment, and subject to negotiation before conclusion and execution. The agreement may be in Khmer and/or in English, but is required to be presented to the SECC and CSX as a supporting document in Khmer.

In cases where a Debt Securities Offering to Qualified Investors is underwritten by a number of underwriters, including those selling the securities to nonresident investors in markets other than Cambodia, the governing law of the underwriting agreement may be chosen in line with the targeted market or investor universe.

d.   General Service Contracts

In the context of a corporate debt securities issuance in Cambodia, including an AMBIF issuance, the issuer may be required to appoint a number of other service providers for specific functions mandated by the SECC (see Chapter III for details). These include a cash settlement agent; a credit rating agency (CRA); and a securities registrar, transfer and paying agent licensed or accredited by the SECC. The issuer will typically also have established relationships with an audit firm and legal counsel; the audit and law firms have to be accredited by the SECC for services to participants in the securities sector.

These service providers normally enter into a general service contract with the issuer, the contents of which are determined by the service provision, the issuer's specific requirements, and applicable prescriptions in laws and regulations, including those outside the securities sector. The contract is typically provided by the service provider and likely subject to negotiation between issuer and service provider before conclusion and execution. The abovementioned services already exist in Cambodia, and a number of service providers are already licensed or accredited with the SECC—with the exception of CRAs. As such, the respective service contracts are typically already in use in the market.

Since these service providers are domestic entities in Cambodia, the expected language of the service contracts is Khmer. In the absence of a domestic CRA in Cambodia, the service contract with an international CRA (if so appointed) would likely be in English.

The service contracts with a CRA and a securities registrar are designated supporting documents for the issuance application to the SECC and the listing application to CSX, including when using the SSF as the application document. On the other hand, the service contract or agreement with the cash settlement agent, auditor, and law firm are prerequisites for an issuance of debt securities since the SECC requires confirmations, opinions, or statements from these parties (termed "experts" in regulations) as supporting documents to an issuance application.

D.   Credit Rating

As part of a comprehensive set of measures to launch the corporate bond market, the SECC introduced the Prakas on Accreditation of Credit Rating Agency in August 2017. This regulation addresses the eligibility criteria and requirements for CRAs to operate in Cambodia, including international entities.

Publicly offered debt securities will need to carry a credit rating from an accredited CRA in Cambodia. A credit rating is required if the issue is a plain or secured bond. If the issue is a guaranteed bond, a credit rating on the issue is not required, but the guarantor of the bond needs to be rated.

In case no CRA has been accredited by the SECC, the issuer shall submit a report on the level of ratios—such as profitability and cash flow ratio, leverage ratio, coverage ratio, and other such applicable ratios—together with a certification of their appropriateness from the underwriter or the experts appointed by the issuer.

Under the Debt Securities Offering to Qualified Investors concept, the SECC allows the need for a credit rating to be set by the parties involved. However, it has been observed in other markets that market participants may still prefer to have credit ratings in place since many market participants designated as professional investors (Qualified Investors in Cambodia) may not be able to replicate in-house the credit assessment process undertaken by the CRAs.

E.   Offering Methods

Underwriters or issuing agents for Debt Securities Offerings to Qualified Investors need not conduct a formal book-building exercise during the placement of the debt securities. This is to avoid the appearance of advertisements for such Debt Securities Offerings to Qualified Investors, which would automatically trigger a full public offering.

Inquiries and reverse inquiries are seen as the likely offering methods for Debt Securities Offerings to Qualified Investors in Cambodia.

F.   Transfer Restrictions

Under the prescriptions of the SECC for Debt Securities Offerings to Qualified Investors, only Qualified Investors may be offered debt securities issued under this concept, and they may only transfer these debt securities to other Qualified Investors.

Pursuant to the Prakas on Debt Securities Offering to Qualified Investors, published on 5 May 2020, the issuer of such debt securities will need to specifically state this transfer restriction in the disclosure document and also provide a corresponding statement to the SECC in the application documents when seeking issuance approval. While the Prakas states the term "transfer restrictions," the practical application equates to selling and transfer restrictions for Qualified Investors.

All investors in the Cambodian securities market will need to obtain an investor ID prior to commencing their buying of securities (see also section G). Institutional Investors are distinguished through a separate application form from individual investors and by the need to supply constituting documents. The distinction as an Institutional Investor (i.e., one category of the Qualified Investors concept) and documentation will remain on file with securities firms used by the investors. As such, the classification of Institutional Investors is possible upon transactions through their investor ID, name, and underlying documentation.

Securities firms executing trades on behalf of Institutional Investors will need to ascertain when carrying out transactions that these transactions are indeed for Institutional Investors by verifying the investor ID. This is supported by the inclusion of the investor ID in the transaction dataset from trade to settlement.

G.   Note Issuance Program

AMBIF promotes the medium-term note (MTN) program, or the note issuance program, format because it not only gives funding flexibility to issuers, but it also represents a common format of bond issuance in the international bond market. This means that potential issuers as well as investors and intermediaries are likely to be familiar with the note issuance programs and related practices in ASEAN+3 markets. Hence, this would make AMBIF comparable to the relevant practices of the international bond market. At the same time, it is expected that potential issuers can benefit from reusing or adopting existing documentation and information disclosure. The SSF already supports multiple issuances.

At this stage, the issuance of domestic bonds or notes to professional investors via an MTN or note issuance program is not evident in the Cambodian market. However, at the time of the compilation of these Implementation Guidelines, the SECC was in the process of evaluating the practical use of an MTN or note issuance program, or a shelf-registration program (for public offerings).

H.   Bondholders Representative

The bondholders representative represents the interests of bondholders in the event of default or bankruptcy of the issuer, or other disputes between investors and issuer, and monitors the condition of the issuer and the issued debt securities through their life cycle. The bondholders representative is required to report to bondholders such status at least every 6 months.

The function of the bondholders representative was introduced in the Prakas on Accreditation of Bondholders Representative, published by the SECC in August 2017. As the title of the *Prakas* suggests, a bondholders representative needs to be accredited by the SECC to carry out said function. Eligible entities are commercial or custodian banks; securities firms; and securities registrars, securities transfer and paying agents. The term accreditation is used since eligible entities are already licensed by the SECC to undertake corresponding business in the securities market; in the case of banks, they are licensed by the NBC.

An accreditation as bondholders representative is valid for 3 years and may be renewed via application to the SECC at least 45 days before the expiry of the current accreditation term.

The appointment of a bondholders representative is mandatory for the issuance of nongovernment (corporate) debt securities via a public offering and Debt Securities Offerings to all Qualified Investors, but not mandatory for Debt Securities Offerings to Qualified Investors if limited to the Institutional Investor category.

I.   Investor Identification

All investors—both domestic and foreign—need to obtain an investor ID prior to investing in the Cambodian securities market. The only distinction between domestic and foreign investors is an indicator in the actual ID ("D" or "F" for domestic or foreign, respectively). The investor ID is used as a distinct identifier in transactions and the securities accounts at CSX (see also next section).

Investors may apply directly to the SECC or through their securities firms. Institutional investors—including those eligible as Qualified Investors—need to fill out Application Form B (Application Form A is for individual investors) and attach their company license, company registration certificate (or equivalent), articles of association, identification card (Cambodian citizens) or passport details (foreigners), and photos of the responsible officers, as well as a power of attorney in their favor.

The necessary steps on how to become an investor in the Cambodian securities market are well explained in the Investor Guide, which is downloadable from the SECC website.[8] Application Form B is also available for download from the SECC website.[9]

The SECC issues a notice to the market in case the contents of the form or the application or approval procedure changes. These notices are also viewable on the CSX website in the News and Publications section.

J.   Asset Safekeeping

The SECC issued the Prakas on the Accreditation of the Custodian Agent in the Securities Sector (Prakas No. 002/2018/SECC/Pr.K.) in May 2018 to facilitate the creation of a dedicated custodian function in the Cambodian securities market.

---

[8] See http://csx.com.kh/news/brochure/viewPost.do?MNCD=7040&postId=86.
[9] See http://csx.com.kh/news/notice/viewPost.do?MNCD=8020&postId=242#.WBw4BktSgpE.

A custodian agent may be a bank or the operator of the securities depository of CSX. In the case of a commercial bank, a no objection letter from the NBC must be obtained prior to application.

For operational reasons, the custodian agent will have to be a member of the securities depository operated by CSX. CSX itself is also mentioned as an eligible custodian agent in the *Prakas*.

Since the application and approval of custodian agents by the SECC, and the establishment of such custodian agent functions in successful applicant(s), may take some time, these Implementation Guidelines will explain the present asset safekeeping practices in the Cambodian securities market, with a view to alleviating concerns of potential investors as to the safety and protection of their holdings.

1.   Current Intermediaries

The current intermediaries in the Cambodian bond market consist of two groups, the securities firms as trading members of the exchange and the so-called CSX "participants." Both types of intermediaries play a role in the settlement process for debt instrument transactions.

CSX participants presently refer to the cash settlement agents (CSAs) who facilitate the settlement of the cash leg of a settlement in CSX. There are presently four CSA participants in CSX.[10]

Once custodian agents have been approved by the SECC, these custodian agents will also become CSX participants.

2.   Account Identification and Segregation of Assets

Securities firms will open one securities account for proprietary trading and holdings, and one client account with subaccounts for each of their investor clients in CSX Depository. The client account and its subaccounts are not part of the securities firm's holdings. Investor holdings are clearly identifiable through the name of the securities subaccount. In addition, through their account opening documentation, securities firms indemnify their investor clients against misuse of their holdings.

Securities firms will also open and maintain cash accounts with one of the CSAs: one for proprietary cash balances ("principal account") and a so-called "client money account," which is an omnibus account to facilitate cash settlement for client transactions. CSAs consider any balances in the client money account as belonging to investors. Securities firms will instruct their CSA to transfer funds for the settlement of investors' securities transactions based on client orders. A corresponding request to the CSA from the operator of CSX Depository ensures that no cash transfer occurs without an underlying securities transaction.

In turn, investors will open a cash account, typically with one of the CSAs participating in CSX Depository. This is intended to allow the securities firm to check the cash account balance prior to placing a purchase order on CSX (see also next section). Investors fund their purchases by instructing the CSA to transfer funds from their own cash account to the client money account of the securities firm placing orders on their behalf. Securities firms do not have direct access to the cash account of their investor clients.

---

[10] The list of CSX participants, including CSAs, is available from the CSX website at http://csx.com.kh/en/member/participants.jsp?MNCD=10512.

The securities account number in CSX is a randomly assigned number, while the investor ID becomes part of the securities subaccount identification. The cash account number is assigned by the CSA of the investor.

3.   Central Records Access at Cambodia Securities Exchange Depository

CSX Depository provides securities safekeeping and settlement records to its securities firm members in the form of system access to securities accounts under each securities firm's purview in the depository database. System access is separated for the proprietary account and client accounts of each securities firm, and subject to an audit trail. Securities firms may not transfer assets out of a client account unless a client instruction has been recorded.

In addition, CSX offers the viewing of the cash balances of each investor as a service to its members. The cash balances are uploaded into CSX Depository at the end of each business day by the CSAs—with any cash settlement for the current day added to the previous day's cash balance by CSX—to be able to show a current cash balance. The cash balances are for viewing purposes only and are not part of the legal records of CSX; no cash transfers can be initiated through this viewing function. Securities firms need to check the cash balance of an investor client prior to placing orders.[11]

4.   Introduction of Custodian Agent

The Prakas for the Accreditation of the Custodian Agent in the Securities Sector (Prakas No. 002/18 SECC/Pr.K.) was promulgated by the SECC on 29 May 2018 and introduced the function of a dedicated custodian—referred to as custodian agent in the Prakas—to the Cambodian securities market.

Custodian agents may be commercial banks, owing to the requirement to conduct foreign exchange transactions for investor clients, which is principally only available under a banking license. However, the operator of the securities depository of CSX is also mentioned in the Prakas as an institution eligible to be a custodian agent. Custodian agents need to be accredited with the SECC following an application process. The accreditation has no expiry or renewal date.[12]

The Prakas prescribes that custodian agents are subject to a number of eligibility criteria for the institution and its staff, and it defines obligations and service principles for the custodian agent. The provisions include that the custodian agent should open custody accounts in the names of the investors and prohibit comingling of the client assets with the custodian agent's own assets.

Please also see section C.2 in this chapter for the custody agreement applicable in this context—referred to as client agreement in the Prakas—and related practices.

K.   Foreign Exchange

Under the Prakas for the Accreditation of the Custodian Agent in the Securities Sector, investors using the services of a custodian agent in Cambodia are required to carry out all foreign exchange transactions via their appointed custodian agent.

---

[11] In principle, investors may open a cash account with any bank in Cambodia to fund their purchases by remitting required cash amounts to the securities firm's client money account at the appropriate time. However, if the account is not opened with a CSA, the securities firm will not be able to check the cash balance of the investor through CSX and, hence, it may result in the investor having to fully prefund any trades.

[12] The term "accreditation" is used by the SECC to indicate that applicants already have an underlying business license for their market activities.

III

AMBIF Bond and Note Issuance Process in Cambodia

Effective August 2017, the SECC started setting specific regulatory processes for the issuance of nongovernment debt securities (corporate bonds) via a public offering and for the related prescriptions for credit ratings and the appointment of a bondholders representative for such issuances.

In May 2020, the SECC promulgated the Prakas on Debt Securities Offering to Qualified Investors as a measure to promote the issuance of corporate bonds to a professional investor market segment. The *Prakas* adopts concise disclosure requirements, being a concession from full-disclosure requirements and a number of other concessions, but it also references definitions and prescriptions established by the SECC in the Prakas on Public Offering of Debt Securities, 2017.

The regulatory processes explained in this chapter focus on Debt Securities Offerings to Qualified Investors and their specific prescriptions only.

A.   Overview of the Regulatory Process

1.   Regulatory Process by Corporate Issuer Type

Table 2 provides an overview of the regulatory process by issuer type and identifies which regulatory authority or market institution is involved. To make the issuance process by issuer type more comparable across ASEAN+3 markets, the table features common issuer type distinctions that are evident in regional markets. Not all markets will distinguish between all such issuer types or prescribe specific approvals.

Table 2: Authorities Involved in the Regulatory Process
by Corporate Issuer Type

Type of Corporate Issuer	SECC	NBC	CSX (listing only)
Resident issuer			
Resident nonfinancial institution	X		X
Resident financial institution	X	X	X
Resident issuing FCY-denominated debt securities	X	(X)[a]	X
Nonresident issuer			
Nonresident nonfinancial institution	N.A.	N.A.	N.A.
Nonresident financial institution	N.A.	N.A.	N.A.
Nonresident issuing FCY-denominated debt securities	N.A.	N.A.	N.A.

CSX = Cambodia Securities Exchange, FCY = foreign currency, NBC = National Bank of Cambodia, N.A. = not applicable, SECC = Securities and Exchange Commission of Cambodia.
[a] The NBC may or may not require approval or consent, in principle, for issuance in foreign currency.
Source: ABMF SF1.

The table reflects the current regulatory regime, which requires approval for the issuance of nongovernment (corporate) debt securities from the SECC and the establishment of listing eligibility and separate listing approval from CSX for debt securities to be listed. Domestic financial institutions require a no objection letter from the NBC prior to issuing debt securities.

Nonresident issuers are presently not (yet) able to issue bonds and notes—or securities, in general—in Cambodia, regardless of the issuance currency.

2.   Regulatory Process Map—Overview

The regulatory process map shown in the figure provides an overview of the regulatory processes relevant for Debt Securities Offerings to Qualified Investors in the Cambodian bond market. While the general process of submitting an application to (and seeking approval from) the SECC is the same, there are distinctive differences in the regulatory processes between public offers and Debt Securities Offerings to Qualified Investors. In these AMBIF Implementation Guidelines, only the regulatory process for Debt Securities Offerings to Qualified Investors has been described in detail. For a comprehensive description of the regulatory process for public offers in the Cambodian market, please refer to the *ASEAN+3 Bond Market Guide for Cambodia*.[13]

---

[13] See https://www.adb.org/publications/asean3-bond-market-guide-2018-cambodia.

Figure: Regulatory Process Map—Overview

Underwriter (if appointed)

Issuer

6
Listing
Approval

2
Confirmation
of Listing
Eligibility

4
Approval and
Registration of
Disclosure
Document

3
Issuance
Application

7
Issuance
Report

1
Request for
Confirmation
of Listing
Eligibility

5
Application
for Listing

SECC

CSX

CSX = Cambodia Securities Exchange, SECC = Securities and Exchange Commission of Cambodia.
Source: ABMF SF1.

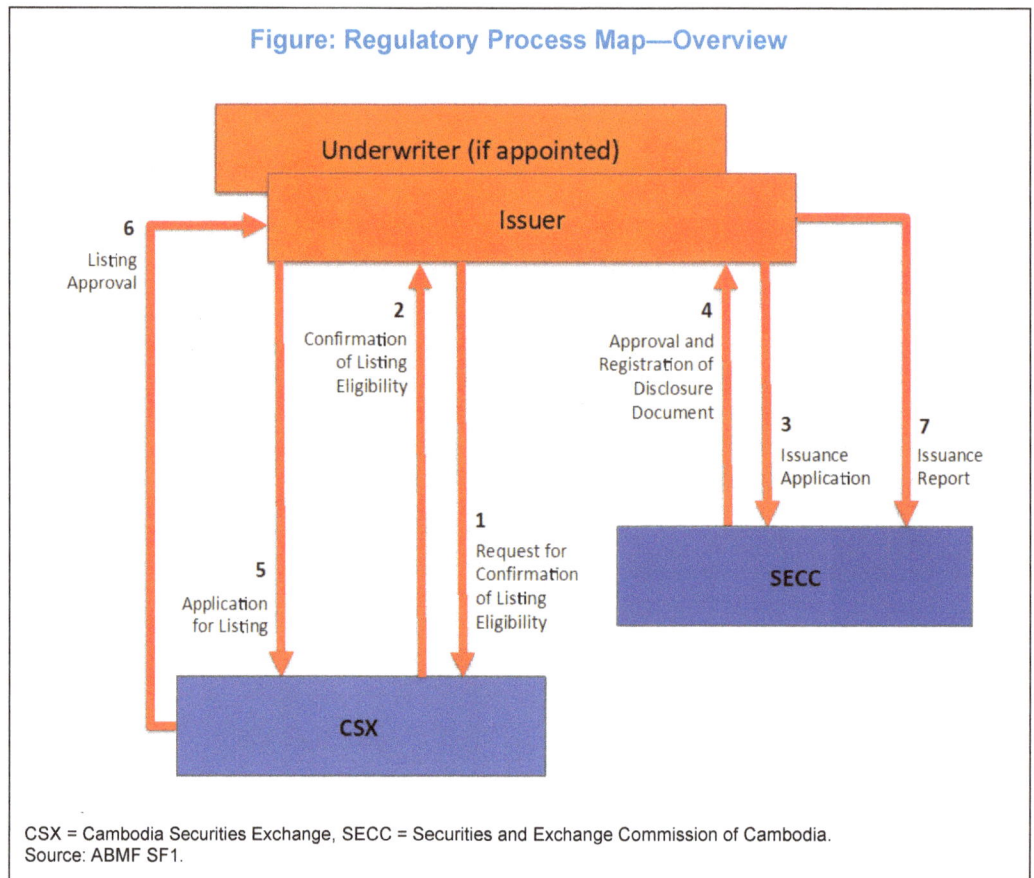

Debt Securities Offerings to Qualified Investors are subject to the approval of the SECC and the registration of the disclosure document. Also, for Debt Securities Offerings to Qualified Investors, the issuer must appoint an underwriter licensed by the SECC.

Debt Securities Offerings to Qualified Investors only require the appointment of a bondholders representative if the offering is exclusively to Qualified Investors (including High-Net Worth Investors); however, if an offering is only aimed at Institutional Investors, the appointment of a bondholders representative is voluntary. At the same time, depending on the type of Qualified Investors (Institutional Investors) the issuer is targeting, appointing a bondholders representative may be a practical consideration, in particular if certain investor types require such a feature under their mandate or prudential regulations.

In the context of issuances under AMBIF, the listing of the debt securities on CSX will be mandatory to fulfill the AMBIF Element of regular disclosure and access to updated information at any time (see Chapter I.3).

B. Issuance Process for Bonds Denominated in Local Currency

This section describes the issuance processes for bonds and notes denominated in Cambodian riel and aimed at Qualified Investors (Debt Securities Offerings to Qualified Investors) in Cambodia.

In the case that regulatory authorities make distinctions according to particular corporate issuer types, such distinctions would be highlighted in the individual sections that follow.

In some cases, bonds or notes issued by a foreign government or government-linked agency may require specific SECC approval, and may also be subject to additional approvals, as the case may be, that are not detailed in these Implementation Guidelines.

1. Issuance Process for Resident Issuer (Other Than Financial Institution)

A potential resident issuer needs to be a public limited company or other legal entity permitted by the SECC. Eligibility criteria for potential issuers are set out in Article 7 of the Prakas on Debt Securities Offering to Qualified Investors, including the minimum number of years of financial statements (including any concessions for listed entities), strong corporate governance, and credit rating requirements.

The issuer needs to appoint a cash settlement agent that is accredited by the SECC, typically a commercial bank, which needs to certify the opening of a separate bank account for the deposit of the issuance proceeds from the Debt Securities Offering to Qualified Investors. The issuer also needs to appoint a securities registrar, securities transfer and paying agent. The service providers, including a bondholders representative and law firm, need to be accredited by or registered with the SECC.

If the issuer wishes to issue a guaranteed bond via a Debt Securities Offering to Qualified Investors, the guarantor will need to be accredited by the SECC and rated by a CRA accredited by the SECC.

The necessary steps to complete the regulatory process are described in detail below.

Step 1—Application for Listing Eligibility Review to the Cambodia Securities Exchange

This step is required for applicants that have not previously had their equity or debt securities listed on a permitted securities market such as CSX. Provisions in Article 9 of the Prakas on Debt Securities Offering to Qualified Investors exempt listed issuers from the need to obtain a confirmation of listing eligibility.

Proposed issuers that do not have an active listing on CSX will need to submit an application for listing eligibility review to CSX. Confirmation of listing eligibility is a prerequisite for the application for issuance to the SECC. The prescriptions for the listing eligibility review are contained in the Debt Securities Listing Rules of CSX.

The application to CSX (shown for a nonlisted issuer) must comprise the following information and documents:

i. general information, including
    a. name of the debt listing applicant in Khmer and Latin,
    b. address of the debt listing applicant,
    c. date of incorporation of the debt listing applicant, and
    d. business objectives of the debt listing applicant;
ii. a copy of the articles of incorporation of the debt listing applicant;
iii. a copy of the certificate of business registration;
iv. a copy of the certificate of tax registration and patent;
v. a copy of business licenses from the relevant authorities;

    vi.   a copy of a letter authorizing a representative of the applicant for the debt listing and the ID of the representative;

   vii.   shareholder information;

  viii.   corporate governance information;

    ix.   information about the business position of the debt listing applicant, consisting of business information and risk factors;

    x.   information about the financial position of the debt listing applicant, consisting of
- a. information about the financial position including all debt and equity securities and profitability,
- b. an asset valuation and/or asset re-valuation (if any), and
- c. audited financial statements as prescribed by the SECC;

    xi.   a credit rating report issued by a CRA accredited by the SECC and/or a report on profitability and cash flow ratio, leverage ratio, and coverage ratio, with certification of the appropriateness from its experts or underwriter in case a CRA does not yet exist in Cambodia;

   xii.   information on the collateral in case of a secured bond;

  xiii.   information on the guarantor—including general information, a credit rating report on the guarantor, and a guarantee agreement—in the case of a guaranteed bond;

  xiv.   information about the debt securities to be listed:
- a. resolution of the board of directors of the debt listing applicant on the debt securities issuance;
- b. specifications of the debt securities to be listed, including
  - i. coupon rate and payment schedule,
  - ii. face value,
  - iii. issuance and maturity date, and
  - iv. allotment method;
- c. the plan of utilizing the proceeds from the debt securities issuance; and
- d. a copy of the Bondholders Representative Agreement; and

   xv.   other information relevant to the listing eligibility review.

During the listing eligibility review, CSX may ask the issuer or underwriter for additional information that it deems material to its decision-making process.

CSX accepts the SSF as key disclosure document for the listing eligibility review. The issuer or underwriter may submit draft or working copy versions of the key disclosure document, such as the SSF, and other supporting documents in English. Legally binding contracts and other material information are required to be submitted in Khmer.

Issuers with equity already listed on CSX need not provide some of the stipulated information and documents if such information has been updated with CSX. CSX will consider providing this concession to issuers with listed debt securities in the future.

Step 2—Result of Listing Eligibility Review from the Cambodia Securities Exchange

CSX will review the listing eligibility of the applicant and provide a result to the issuer within 10 working days from the receipt of the completed application. If the issuer is an equity-listed entity, the review period will only be 3 working days. The result notification will be in Khmer and in writing.

Should CSX reject the application, it will provide reasons for such rejection. In such cases, the issuer may seek clarification from CSX for the rejection or appeal to the SECC for a further review and decision.

Step 3—Issuance Application to the Securities and Exchange Commission of Cambodia

The issuer (also termed "applicant" in the regulations) will need to submit an application to the SECC in a form to be prescribed by the SECC.[14] The application, which needs to be in writing, consists of a number of components that are further detailed below. The issuer may secure the help of the underwriter or securities firm (if appointed) for the compilation of the application and its constituent parts. While the issuer retains overall responsibility for the content of the application and the disclosure document, service providers, including the underwriter or securities firm (also termed "experts" in the regulations), will be responsible for statements attributed to (and information provided by) them.

The following documents will need to be submitted:

i. the SSF as the key application and disclosure document, with the minimum contents prescribed by the SECC;

ii. supporting documents as attachments, including
    a. a certified copy of the certificate of incorporation;
    b. a certificated copy of the articles of association;
    c. the board of directors' resolution on the debt securities offering to Qualified Investors;
    d. a letter from a commercial bank, acting as a cash settlement agent, certifying the opening of a separate account for the proceeds from the debt securities offering to Qualified Investors;
    e. a due diligence report issued by the underwriter licensed by the SECC (if appointed);
    f. a due diligence report issued by a lawyer accredited by the SECC;
    g. a certified copy of an underwriting agreement or an engagement letter in case the applicant has not yet signed an agreement with the underwriter (if appointed);
    h. a certified copy of the agreement with the securities registrar, securities transfer and paying agent;
    i. a credit rating report issued by a CRA accredited by the SECC (if any);
    j. a certified copy of the agreement with a CRA (if any);
    k. a certified copy of the agreement with a bondholders representative (if appointed);
    l. material agreements (if any);
    m. a statement on transfer restrictions;
    n. documents confirming the tax duty compliance;
    o. in case the applicant wishes to issue secured bonds to Qualified Investors, the applicant shall include the following additional documents:
        i. evidence of the collateral;
        ii. certificate from the related authority, which states that the collateral is free from any lien; and
        iii. a report on the asset valuation issued by a valuation company accredited by the SECC;
    p. in case the applicant wishes to issue guaranteed bonds to Qualified Investors, the applicant shall include the following additional documents:
        i. a credit rating report on the guarantor issued by a CRA accredited by the SECC (unless otherwise determined by the Director General of the SECC), and
        ii. the guarantee agreement; and
    q. other documents as required by the Director General of the SECC.

---

[14] At present, the SECC does not define the form or format of the application. It can consider any form or format, such as the SSF, on its merits.

The application and key disclosure document (i.e., the SSF) shall be signed by a person authorized to sign on behalf of the applicant. Presently, the SECC requires the final version of the application form and the SSF to be submitted in Khmer.

The issuer must also provide proof of the eligibility of its debt securities for listing on CSX (see Step 1) and of the acceptance by CSX of its intended pricing.

Article 11 of the Prakas on Debt Securities Offering to Qualified Investors contains the minimum contents of the disclosure document. The SECC considers the SSF as fulfilling these contents requirements. A link to the SSF in its latest version is provided in Appendix 1 of these Implementation Guidelines and the SSF may be amended if the SECC's requirements change in future.

The disclosure document (SSF) needs to have the following minimum contents:

i.   a statement on the transfer restrictions,
ii.   the summary of the disclosure document,
iii.   information about the debt securities offering,
iv.   information about the use of proceeds,
v.   general information about the applicant and its operation,
vi.   information about risk factors,
vii.   information about corporate governance,
viii. financial information and/or consolidated financial information, and
ix.   the components of the annex.

The disclosure document shall contain the following statement: "All information in the disclosure document is under the responsibility of the issuer and the entities related to the preparation of this disclosure document."

The annex to the disclosure document (SSF) needs to comprise the following components:

i.   detailed terms and conditions of the debt securities,
ii.   financial report audited by an independent auditor,
iii.   interim financial statement reviewed by the independent auditor (if any),
iv.   summary credit rating report issued by a CRA accredited by the SECC (if any),
v.   asset valuation report (if any),
vi.   summary credit rating report on the guarantor issued by a CRA accredited by the SECC (in case of guaranteed bond issuance), and
vii.   experts' consent letter on establishing their statement or report in the disclosure document.

The application to the SECC will need to be accompanied by payment of a fee for the review and registration of the disclosure document by the SECC. The fee is not refundable even if the application is not successful.

Step 4—Review and Approval from the Securities and Exchange Commission of Cambodia and Registration of the Disclosure Document

The SECC will review the application and disclosure document (SSF) and supporting documents, and may ask, in writing, for additional information or the replacement of information in the disclosure document and supporting documents, as the case may be. In such a case, the issuer (and its service providers) has 15 working days from the day the request has been issued to respond to the SECC's request, or any other time period that the SECC may specify, after which the application would either become void or the validity would be extended if there is a reasonable explanation by the applicant for the delay.

The SECC will inform the issuer in writing of its approval or rejection of the issuance application and the registration of the disclosure document within 30 working days from the receipt of complete documentation. The approval and registration are valid for 6 months.

In case of rejection, the SECC will provide the applicable reasons for which the application was rejected, which may include incomplete, false, or misleading statements; the status of the issuer; or qualifications of a party acting for the issuing company. The reasons for a possible rejection are outlined in Article 16 of the Prakas on Debt Securities Offering to Qualified Investors.

Once the SECC has issued its approval and registration of the disclosure document, the issuer is able to offer the debt securities to Qualified Investors.

Step 5—Subscription of Debt Securities

Once the SECC has approved the issuance of debt securities and registered the disclosure document, the issuer may proceed with the Debt Securities Offering to Qualified Investors within the validity of the disclosure document (6 months), starting with the subscription. The subscription is open to Qualified Investors only.

The subscription shall be conducted through a securities firm or firms licensed by the SECC. There is no specified time frame for the subscription to a Debt Securities Offering to Qualified Investors; while a period of 4 days has emerged as the typical length of a subscription period, the underwriter determines the actual period. The subscription form to be used will be determined by the SECC and will need to include the disclosure document.

The securities firm(s) will need to issue a receipt and deposit any subscription moneys received into the dedicated account with the cash settlement agent; subscriber information will be kept by the securities registrar appointed by the issuer. When the subscription is completed, the issuer shall submit a report on the subscription result to the SECC without delay. The completion report will need to include a confirmation from the cash settlement agent on the proceeds received from the subscription.

The issuer, securities registrar, or securities firm(s) shall distribute the debt securities to successful subscribers by the next working day following the closing date of the subscription period. The issuer will need to deposit the debt securities issued with the securities depository operator for the debt securities to become tradable.

In the event that the debt securities remain unsubscribed at the end of the subscription period, the underwriter (if any) shall subscribe to the remaining debt securities in line with its contractual agreement, and the issuer needs to submit a report on the subscription of the remaining debt securities to the SECC without delay and in a form determined by the SECC.

If the subscription of the debt securities fails, the registered disclosure document may be cancelled. In case of an unsuccessful subscription, provisions for the refund of subscription amounts are stated in Articles 21 and 22 of the Prakas.

Step 6—Listing of Debt Securities

The approval from the SECC and the registration of the disclosure document is the prerequisite for the completion of the listing process of debt securities on CSX. At the same time, the listing of debt securities is an integral part of the issuance process under AMBIF (see Chapter I.3).

Once the issuer has obtained the issuance approval from the SECC (for a Debt Securities Offering to Qualified Investors) and the confirmation of the registration of the disclosure document, and the subscription process has been completed, the issuer shall complete the listing application process within 7 working days. The listing process is described in the Debt Securities Listing Rules of CSX, which are available in English from the CSX website.[15]

At the time of the listing application, the issuer needs to fulfill the following criteria:

    i.   the shareholders' equity of the applicant shall be at least KHR2 billion, except in the case of a secured bond;
    ii.   the total nominal value of the issued debt securities and to-be-listed debt securities shall be at least KHR1 billion, or at least KHR500 million for a secured bond;
    iii.   the face value of the debt securities shall be KHR100,000; and
    iv.   all issued debt securities shall be deposited at the operator of the securities depository of CSX.

The issuer will need to submit a Listing Application Form to CSX, with the documents attached as mentioned below:

    i.   the disclosure document (such as the SSF) already registered with the SECC;
    ii.   documents proving the debt securities subscription settlement;
    iii.   a letter confirming that the debt securities have been deposited at the operator of the securities depository (i.e., CSX Depository);
    iv.   a debt securities allotment report;
    v.   a copy of the bondholder representative agreement or the agreement with the registrar, transfer and paying agent; and
    vi.   a copy of the underwriting agreement.

The Listing Application Form is a physical document available from CSX and is to be submitted in duplicate. The form contains text in Khmer and English, but it is required to be completed in Khmer only. Legally binding contracts and other material information will need to be submitted in Khmer. CSX accepts the SSF when registered with the SECC; the SSF will be in Khmer as per current SECC requirements.

The issuer will need to sign a Securities Listing Agreement with CSX, in a format approved by the SECC, prior to listing; the agreement will take effect on the effective listing date.

CSX will check on the status of the issuer—based on its due diligence at the time of the Listing Eligibility Review—and respond within 5 working days with its listing approval and the effective listing date information. The listing approval will be in writing in Khmer in the form of a physical letter to the issuer.

A listing fee will be payable by the issuer prior to the effective listing date (please see the relevant details in Chapter VI of the *ASEAN+3 Bond Market Guide for Cambodia*).

Step 7—Post-Issuance Reporting Obligations

When the issuance of debt securities to Qualified Investors is completed, the issuer is required to report the result of the offer without delay to the SECC; this report needs to include a confirmation from the cash settlement agent on the proceeds from the subscription. Detailed provisions on the timely and continuous disclosure of material

---

[15] See http://csx.com.kh/laws/lsr/listPosts.do?MNCD=20501.

events are stipulated in Article 27 of the Prakas on Debt Securities Offering to Qualified Investors, with further provisions on periodic disclosure in Article 28. The need for the issuer to advise the SECC of a planned change in bondholders representative is separately prescribed in Article 31.

The issuer will also need to comply with disclosure provisions in the CSX Debt Securities Listing Rules and the Prakas on Corporate Disclosure.

2.   Issuance Process for Resident Financial Institution

Banks and financial institutions supervised by the NBC are required to seek a no objection letter from the NBC for the issuance and subsequent listing of debt securities on CSX. According to the Prakas on Listing Criteria of Banking and Financial Institutions on Cambodia Securities Exchange, published by the NBC in September 2017, additional criteria apply such as an institution's net worth and the assessment grade given by the NBC.

The actual issuance application and approval process is the same as for all other resident issuers (see section 1).

3.   Issuance Process for Nonresident Issuer

In the absence of specific provisions in *Kram* or *Prakas* for the securities market, nonresidents are not yet able to issue debt securities in the Cambodian market.

C.   Issuance Process for Bonds Denominated in Foreign Currency

Issuance Process for US Dollar-Denominated Bonds and Notes

The actual issuance and listing application and approval process for US dollar-denominated bonds and notes is the same as for bonds and notes denominated in riels. CSX can list, price, trade, and settle securities in both riels and US dollars.

Appendix 1
Resource Information

For easy reference and access to further information about the topics discussed in the ASEAN+3 Multi-Currency Bond Issuance Framework (AMBIF) Implementation Guidelines for Cambodia—including the relevant policy bodies, regulatory authorities, securities market-related institutions, and the Cambodian bond market at large—interested parties are encouraged to utilize the following links (all websites available in English):

ASEAN+3 Multi-Currency Bond Issuance Framework—Single Submission Form
Available from the ABMF website:
http://tinyurl.com/AMBIF-Single-Submission-Form.

ASEAN+3 Bond Market Guide—Cambodia (2018)
https://asianbondsonline.adb.org/documents/abmf_cam_bond_market_guide_2018.pdf.

AsianBondsOnline (Asian Development Bank)
https://asianbondsonline.adb.org/economy/?economy=KH.

Cambodia Securities Exchange
http://www.csx.com.kh/main.do.

Cambodia Securities Exchange—Debt Securities Listing Rules
http://csx.com.kh/laws/lsr/listPosts.do?MNCD=20501.

Ministry of Economy and Finance [partly in English]
http://www.mef.gov.kh.

National Bank of Cambodia
http://www.nbc.org.kh/english/index.php.

Royal Government of Cambodia—Financial Sector Development Strategy 2011–2020 (an Asian Development Bank publication)
http://adb.org/sites/default/files/pub/2012/financial-sector-development-strategy-2011-2020.pdf.

Securities and Exchange Commission of Cambodia
http://www.secc.gov.kh/english/.

Securities and Exchange Commission of Cambodia—List of Prakas
http://www.secc.gov.kh/english/m23.php?pn=3.

Appendix 2
Glossary of Technical Terms

accreditation	Consent given by the Securities and Exchange Commission of Cambodia (SECC) to institutions already licensed as market participants for specific activities in the securities sector
Anukret	Sub-decree containing regulations or rules pursuant to specific laws (single and plural use)
applicant	Term used for a potential issuer who has filed an application for the issuance of (debt) securities with the SECC
approval	Regulatory consent for market infrastructure operators
bondholders representative	Term used in Cambodia for the function of representing the interests of bondholders in relation to the issuer
Bondholders Representative Agreement	Agreement to be entered into between issuer and bondholders representative
cash settlement agent	A commercial bank receiving issuing proceeds from a bond issuance or settling the cash leg in bond settlement for investors; the bank has to be accredited by the SECC
client agreement	Term used in the Prakas on the Accreditation of the Custodian Agent in the Securities Sector for the custody agreement
client money account	Omnibus cash account maintained by a securities firm with a cash settlement agent for all its investors
custodian agent	Term used in regulations for an eligible entity providing custodian services in the securities sector in Cambodia
custody agreement	Contract governing the service provision between investor and the appointed custodian agent accredited by the SECC (also custodian agreement)
Debt Securities Offerings to Qualified Investors	Issuance method representing the professional bond market in Cambodia; these offers are only available to Qualified Investors
exempt securities transaction	Specific term under the law for securities transactions not subject to licensing as an activity of securities firms or representatives, such as the issuance of government securities
High Net-Worth Investors	Investor category under the Qualified Investors concept, with specific qualifying criteria
Institutional Investors	Investor category under the Qualified Investors concept, with specific legal entities defined
Kram	Law or decree (single and plural use)

licensed	Refers to entities admitted to the securities or financial market in Cambodia (e.g., securities firms are licensed by the SECC and commercial banks by the National Bank of Cambodia)
Listing Approval Form	Physical, official document required by the Cambodia Securities Exchange at the time of the listing application; to be signed by issuer and underwriter
over-the-counter	Organized trading of unlisted securities
permitted securities market	Term used in law and regulations for a market approved by the SECC for the trading of securities, including debt securities
Prakas	Official declarations or notices (from regulatory authorities) that interpret laws and regulations (single and plural use)
private placement	Issuance method defined in law and regulations for offer to no more than 30 investors of any kind, with specific prescriptions for advertising and marketing activities
public company	Does not denote a listed company, as in other markets; instead, it refers to companies that are not classified as private
public investors	Market-specific term for retail or general investors
Qualified Investors	Professional investor concept in Cambodia (Prakas on Qualified Investors in the Securities Sector published in August 2016)
registration	Term used to refer to the lodging with, and acceptance by, the SECC of the disclosure document for debt securities
securities market operator	Official term in legislation and regulations for an exchange or facilitator of an over-the-counter market
securities sector	Official name in Cambodian regulations for the securities market
underwriter	Securities firm licensed by the SECC for the underwriting of securities
underwriting agreement	Contract between issuer and underwriter setting the roles of the underwriter and conditions for the bond issuance

Source: ABMF SF1.

Appendix 3
Applicable Laws and
Regulations

The applicable laws, sub-decrees, and regulations (domestically referred to as *Kram*, *Anukret*, and *Prakas* or Official Declarations, respectively) relevant for the corporate bond market at the time of the compilation of these ASEAN+3 Multi-Currency Bond Issuance Framework (AMBIF) Implementation Guidelines for Cambodia are listed below.

Kram (Laws)

Table A3.1: List of Relevant Kram for the Corporate Bond Market

Designation	Title	Issued by	Last Issued
NS/RKM/100 7/028	Law on the Issuance and Trading of Non-Government Securities	National Assembly	2007
NS/RKM/120 6/036	Law on the Organization and Conduct of the National Bank of Cambodia	National Assembly	2006

Note: The above *Kram* are available on the website of the Securities and Exchange Commission of Cambodia (SECC) at http://www.secc.gov.kh/english/m21.php?pn=3.
Source: ABMF compilation based on SECC information.

Anukret (Sub-decrees)

Table A3.2: List of Relevant Anukret for the Corporate Bond Market

Designation	Title	Issued by	Last Issued
No. 01 ANKR BK	Anukret on Tax Incentives in the Securities Sector	National Assembly	2019
No. 54 ANKR BK	Anukret on the Implementation of the Law on the Issuance and Trading of Non-Government Securities	National Assembly	2009
No. 97 ANKR BK	Anukret on the Conduct and Organization of the Securities and Exchange Commission of Cambodia	National Assembly	2008

Note: The above *Anukret* are available on the website of the Securities and Exchange Commission of Cambodia (SECC) at http://www.secc.gov.kh/english/m22.php?pn=3.
Source: ABMF compilation based on SECC information.

Prakas (Official Declarations—Equivalent to Regulations)

Table A3.3: List of Relevant Prakas for the Corporate Bond Market

Designation	Title	Issued by	Last Issued
No. 006/20 SECC/Pr.K.	Prakas on Debt Securities Offering to Qualified Investors	SECC	2020
No. 007/19 SECC/Pr.K.	Prakas on Fees for Debt Securities Trading	SECC	2019
No. 002/18 SECC/Pr.K.	Prakas on the Accreditation of the Custodian Agent in the Securities Sector	SECC	2018
No. 007/18 K.M.K/BB.K.	Prakas on Corporate Disclosure	SECC	2018
B7.017.300 Prokor	Prakas on Conditions for Banking and Financial Institutions for Application to be Listed on the Cambodia Securities Exchange	NBC	2017
No. 012/17 SECC/Pr.K.	Prakas on Dispute Resolution in Securities Sector	SECC	2017
No. 011/17 SECC/Pr.K.	Prakas on Accreditation of Credit Rating Agency	SECC	2017
No. 010/17 SECC/Pr.K.	Prakas on Accreditation of Bondholders Representative	SECC	2017
No. 009/17 SECC/Pr.K.	Prakas on Public Offering of Debt Securities	SECC	2017
No. 005/16 SECC/Pr.K.	Prakas on Qualified Investors in the Securities Sector	SECC	2016
No. 009/10 SECC/Pr.K.	Prakas on the Registration of Securities Registrar, Securities Transfer Agent and Paying Agent	SECC	2010

NBC = National Bank of Cambodia, SECC = Securities and Exchange Commission of Cambodia.
Notes: The above *Prakas* are available on the website of the SECC at
http://www.secc.gov.kh/english/m23.php?pn=3. *Prakas* issued by the National Bank of Cambodia are
available to view and download at https://www.nbc.org.kh/english/legislation/prakas_new.php.
Source: ABMF compilation based on publicly available information.

Rules of Cambodia Securities Exchange

Table A3.4: List of Relevant Rules for the Corporate Bond Market

Designation	Title	Issued by	Last Issued
No. 004/20 SECC/Pr.K.; No. 019/17 SECC/Pr.K.	Operating Rules of Securities Depository of the Cambodia Securities Exchange	SECC	2020
No. 003/20 SECC/Pr.K.; No. 016/17 SECC/Pr.K.	Debt Securities Listing Rules of the Cambodia Securities Exchange	SECC	2020
No. 002/20 SECC/Pr.K.; No. 003/19 SECC/Pr.K.; No. 017/17 SECC/Pr.K.	Operating Rules of Securities Market of the Cambodia Securities Exchange	SECC	2020
No. 001/19 SECC/Pr.K.; No. 003/11 SECC/Pr.K.	Membership Rules	SECC	2019
No. 018/17 SECC/Pr.K.	Operating Rules of Securities Clearing and Settlement of the Cambodia Securities Exchange	SECC	2017

SECC = Securities and Exchange Commission of Cambodia.
Note: The implementation of rules for the Cambodia Securities Exchange is promulgated via SECC *Prakas*.
Source: Cambodia Securities Exchange. Listing Rules.
http://csx.com.kh/laws/lsr/listPosts.do?MNCD=20501.

www.ingramcontent.com/pod-product-compliance
Lightning Source LLC
Chambersburg PA
CBHW040147200326
41519CB00035B/7621